The Standard

OPALESCENT GLASS

PRICE GUIDE

Bill Edwards

COLLECTOR BOOKS
A Division of Schroeder Publishing Co., Inc.

Searching For A Publisher?

We are always looking for knowledgeable people considered to be experts within their fields. If you feel that there is a real need for a book on your collectible subject and have a large comprehensive collection, contact us.

COLLECTOR BOOKS
P.O. Box 3009
Paducah, Kentucky 42002-3009

Additional copies of this book may be ordered from:

COLLECTOR BOOKS
P.O. Box 3009
Paducah, Kentucky 42002-3009

@$9.95. Add $2.00 for postage and handling.

Copyright: Schroeder Publishing Co., Inc. 1992

This book or any part thereof may not be reproduced without the written consent of the Author and Publisher.

1 2 3 4 5 6 7 8 9 0

Preface

In an attempt to offer the collector a price guide for opalescent glass that is more complete, more up-to-date and broader in scope than any previous guide, I've spent more than a year photographing, handling and studying this glass. As the author of several books dealing with carnival glass, I was surprised at their similarities and found pressed opalescent glass like an old friend; the blown glass was a new area that has proved to be something I am still learning about.

This guide has been designed to supply prices for virtually all shapes and colors catalogued so far. Prices followed by an asterisk (*) are speculative. The same mark (*) after a pattern name indicates the pattern has been reproduced. In a few instances prices have been averaged when several varieties of one shape are known. I have made a concerted effort to list many patterns previously unlisted, including patterns from the 1920's and 1930's as well as British patterns previously ignored. Values were tabulated from dealer's lists, shop taggings, antique guide listings and personal speculation. Auction prices played a minor role due to their seldom giving a true value picture. All items are priced as mint (condition) and complete (American sugars priced with lids, British sugars as open compote shapes). *Please remember prices are only guides and are not etched in stone. As with all guides, it is meant to advise rather than set prices.*

For the most part I've stuck to pattern names established by William Heacock except where another pattern name is more commonly used (sometimes keeping up with all of the name changes proved to be a full-time job).

Finally, let me say I think opalescent glass, especially pressed novelty items, are one of the best buys in collectible glass today and can only grow in value in the near future. In addition, most opalescent rarities are still within reason, price-wise, and can be found on occasion at bargain-basement rates. How long this will be true, no one can say, but certainly opalescent glass has to be a speculator's dream, not only for its present values but for its artistic beauty.

Bill Edwards

Introduction

From its inception in the 1880's opalescent glass has enjoyed a widely receptive audience, both in England where it was introduced and here in America where a young but growing market was ready for any touch of brightness and beauty for the hearth and home.

Early American makers, such as Hobbs, Brockunier and Company (1863–1888), Buckeye Glass (1878–1896), LaBelle Glass (1872–1888), American Glass (1889-1891), Nickel Plate Glass (1888–1893), and of course, the Northwood Glass Company in its various locations (1888 until its demise in 1924) were the primary producers, especially in early blown opalescent glass production. They were not by themselves, of course. Other companies such as Model Flint (1893–1899), Fostoria Shade & Lamp Co. (1890–1894), Consolidated Lamp & Glass (1894–1897), Elson Glass (1882–1893), West Virginia Glass (1893–1896), National Glass (1899–1903), Beaumont Glass (1895–1906), Dugan Glass (1904–1913) which then became Diamond Glass (1914–1931); and finally the Jefferson Glass company (1900–1933) added their talents in all sorts of opalescent items in both blown and pressed glass.

The major production covered 40 years (1880–1920); however beginning shortly after the turn of the century the Fenton Glass Company of Williamstown, West Virginia, joined the ranks of opalescent manufactures and has continued production off and on until the present time. Their production from 1907 to 1940 is an important part of the opalescent field and has been covered to some extent in this price guide. The Fenton factory, along with Dugan and Jefferson glass, produced quality opalescent glass items long after the rest of the companies had ceased operations, primarily in pressed items in patterns they had used for other types of glassware.

To understand just what opalescent glass is has always been easy; to explain the process of making this glass is quite another matter. If the novice will think of two layers of glass, one colored and one clear, that have been fused so that the clear areas become milky when fired a second or third time, the picture of the process becomes easier to see. It is, of course, much more complicated than that but for the sake of clarity, imagine the clear layer being pressed so that the second firing gives this opal milkyness to the outer edges, be they design or the edges themselves and the process becomes clearer. It is, of course, the skill of the glassmaker to control this opalescence so that it does what he wants. It is a fascinating process and anyone who has had the privilege of watching a glassmaker at work can testify to it being a near-miracle.

Today, thousands of collectors seek opalescent glass and each has his or her own favorites. Current markets place blown opalescent glass as more desirable, with cranberry leading the color field, but there are many ways to collect and groupings of one shape or one pattern or even one manufacturer are not uncommon. When you purchase this glass the same rules apply as any other glass collectible: (1) look for any damage and do not pay normal prices for damage; (2) choose good color as well as good milky opalescence; (3) **Buy what pleases you!** You have to live with it, so buy what you like. To care for your glass, wash it carefully in luke-warm water and a mild soap; **Never put old glass in a dishwasher!** Display your glass in an area that is well lighted and enjoy it!

Abalone Handled Bowl 7"
Blue Opalescent

Argonaut Shell Novelty Banana Bowl
Blue Opalescent

Argonaut Shell Sauce
Blue Opalescent

Argonaut Shell (Nautilus)
Novelty Bowl Vaseline

Barbells Bowl
White Opalescent

Basketweave Open Edge Bowl
(Fenton) White Opalescent

Beaded Cable Rose Bowl
Blue Opalescent

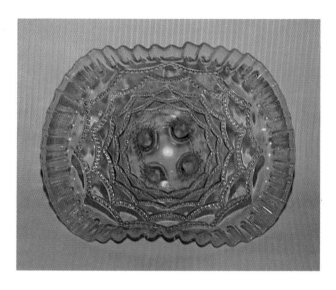

Beaded Drapes Banana Bowl
Blue Opalescent

Beaded Fleur-De-Lis Compote
Blue Opalescent

Beaded Shell Berry Set
Blue Opalescent

Beatty Rib Cigar Tray
(rare and previoulsy unlisted)
Blue Opalescent

Beaded Stars Advertising Plate (rare)
Blue Opalescent

Beatty Swirl Celery Vase
Blue Opalescent

Beatty Swirl Tray
(Variant—40 ribs swirling left rather than right)
Very rare
Blue Opalescent

Button Panels Bowl and Rosebowl
Blue Opalescent

Chick w/Leaf and Scroll Border 7" Plate
Blue Opalescent (Late)

**Christmas Snowflake
(Northwood's)
Water Set (Rare)
White Opalescent**

**Coin Spot Pitcher
Blue Opalescent**

**Coin Spot Water Pitcher
White Opalescent**

**Corn Vase
Blue Opalescent**

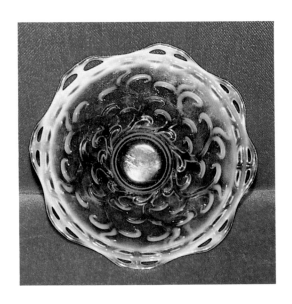

Coral Bowl
Emerald Opal

Diamond and Daisy Bowl
White Opalescent w/Goofus Finish
(previously unlisted pattern)

Diamond and Oval
Thumbprint Vase
Blue Opalescent

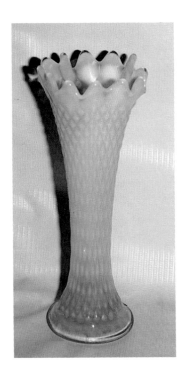

Diamond Point Vase
Blue Opalescent

Diamond Point and Fleur-De-Lis
White Opalescent

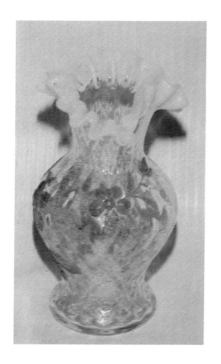

**Divilbis Atomizer
Made by Fenton 1930's
Cobalt Blue**

**Dolphins Compote
Blue Opalescent**

**Diamond Vase Coralene
Decorated (rare)
White Opalescent**

**Dolphins Compote
Canary Opalescent**

**Duncan and Miller Freeform Bowl
1930's
Blue Opalescent**

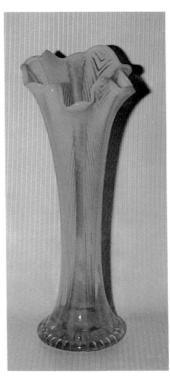

Fancy Fantails Rosebowl
Blue Opalescent

Feathers Vase
Blue Opalescent

Fenton's Hobnail Lamp 1930's
Blue Opalescent

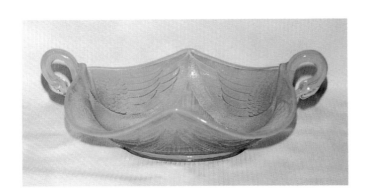

Fenton's Swan Bowl (rare) 1930's
Blue Opalescent

Fishnet Lily (From Epergne)
Emerald Opal

**Flora Novelty Bowl
Cobalt Opalescent**

**Flora Spooner
White Opal**

**Hilltop Vines Novelty
Blue Opalescent**

**Fruit Patch Compote (English)
Canary Opalescent**

**Fluted Scrolls Puff Jar
Blue Opalescent**

**Hobnail Variant w/Zipper Mould
Late Hobnail Pattern
White Opal**

**Hobnail Vase
White Opalescent**

**Honeycomb and Clover Bowl
Blue Opalescent**

**Late Hobnail Spittoon
1930's–1940's
Cranberry Opalescent—Possibly
British**

Interior Panel Fan Vase
Amber Opalescent (Fenton)

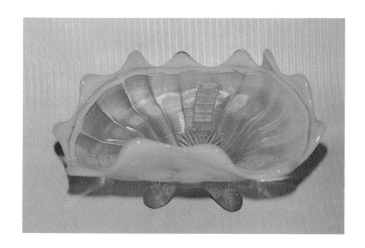

Jackson Novelty Bowl
Blue Opalescent

Jefferson Spool Vase
Green Opalescent

Jefferson Wheel
Blue Opalescent

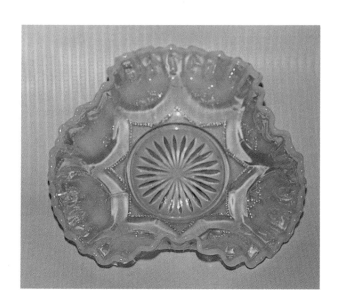

Jeweled Heart Novelty Bowl
Green Opalescent

**Leaf and Beads Novelty Bowl
Blue Opalescent**

**(Bubble) Lattice Bride's Basket
Blue Opalescent**

**Leaf Chalice
Green Opalescent**

**Lined Heart Vase
Blue Opalescent**

**Little Swan (Dugan) Slightly larger
than Northwood version
Green Opalescent**

**Little Swan (Northwood)
Slightly smaller than Dugan version
Blue Opalescent**

**Lorna Vase
Blue Opalescent**

**Many Ribs Vase
Blue Opalescent**

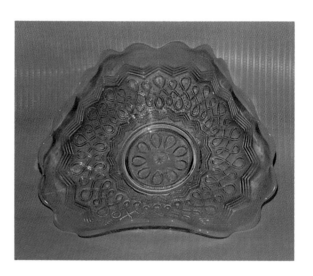

**Many Loops Bowl
White Opalescent**

**Mary Ann Vase (unlisted)
Blue Opalescent**

**Meander Bowl
Blue Opalescent**

**Meander Bowl
Green Opalescent**

**(Northwood) Hobnail
Creamer and Spooner
White Opalescent**

**Northwood's Peacocks (On The Fence)
Blue Opalescent**

**Opal Open Compote (Beaded Panels)
Blue Opalescent**

**Open-Edge Basketweave Bowl
White Opalescence**

**Pearl Flowers
Blue Opalescent**

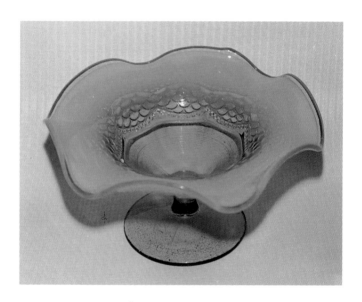

**Pearls and Scales Compote
Emerald Opalescent**

**Pearls and Scales Compote
Vaseline Opalescent**

**Plain Jane Footed Nappy
Blue Opalescent
Previously unlisted**

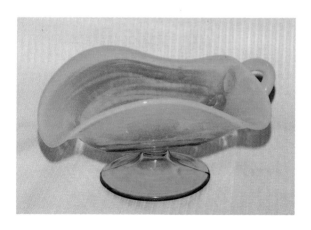

Pressed Coinspot Compote
(Interior View)
Blue Opalescent

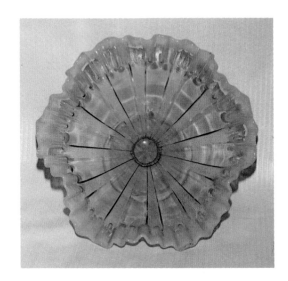

Popsickle Sticks
Footed Bowl
Blue Opalescent

Prince Albert and Victoria Creamer
Canary Opalescent

Princess Diana (English) Creamer
Canary Opalescent

Prince William (English)
Open Sugar and Creamer
Blue Opalescent

Pulled Rib Novelty Bowl
Blue Opalescent
Previously Unreported Pattern
(Possibly Fostoria)

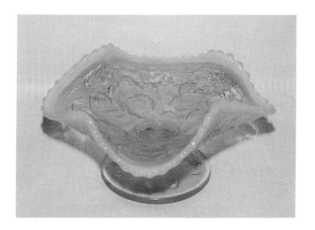

Question Marks Compote w/Georgia Bell
Exterior (previously unlisted opalescent
pattern) Blue Opalescent

Reverse Drapery Vase
White Opalescent

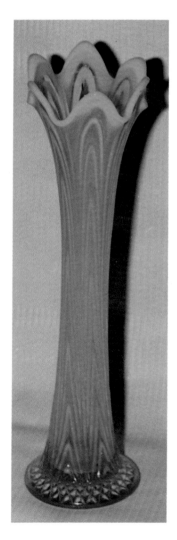

Reverse Drapery Vase
Green Opalescent

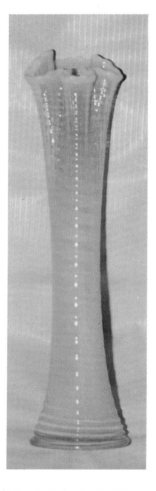

Ribbed Spiral 15" Vase
French Opalescent

Ribbed Spiral Compote (Jelly)
Blue Opalescent

Ribbed Herringbone Pitcher (Very Rare)
White Opal

Ruffles and Rings
Blue Opalescent

Rustic Hobnail Handled Basket (unlisted)
(Pattern found on Northwood's Town Pump)
White Opal Rare

S-Repeat
Blue Opalescent

Shell (Beaded Shell)
Master Bowl
Blue Opal

Shell and Dots Rose Bowl
Blue Opalescent

Spanish Lace Tumbler
Blue Opalescent

**Spokes and Wheels Plate
Blue Opalescent**

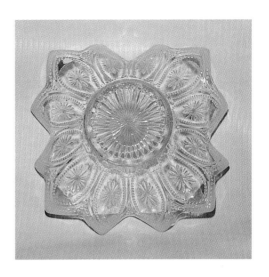

**Spokes and Wheels Square Plate
(Rare Aqua Opalescent color not
previously reported)**

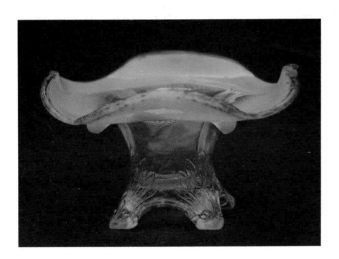

**Swag with Brackets Whimsey
(From footed sugar)
Blue Opalescent with Cranberry Edging.**

**Swirl Vase Fenton 1930's
Green Opalescent**

**Swirling Maze Bowl
White Opalescent**

**Tiny Teardrops Vase
Blue Opalescent**

**Swirling Maze Bowl (Scarce)
Blue Opalescent**

**Tokyo Compote
Blue Opalescent**

**Tokyo Footed Plate
Blue Opalescent**

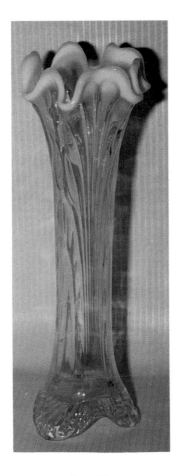

**Tokyo Vase
White Opalescent**

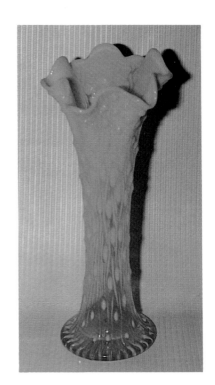

**Treetrunk Vase
Blue Opalescent**

**Vintage Bowl (Northwood)
Goofus Trim
White Opalescent**

**Waffle Pattern Epergne (European)
Olive and Pink Opalescent (rare)**

**Waterlily and Cattails
Bon-Bon (rare shape)
Blue Opalescent**

**Waterlily and Cattails Sauce
Amethyst Opalescent**

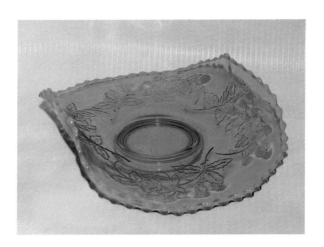

**Wild Rose Banana Plate
(previously unlisted)
Cobalt Opalescent**

**Winter Cabbage Bowl
Green Opalescent**

**Wheel and Block Plate
White Opal with Goofus
Decoration**

**Wild Rose Mug
White Opalescent with
Gold Goofus Paint
(Previoulsy unlisted)**

**William and Mary (English)
Creamer
Canary Opalescent**

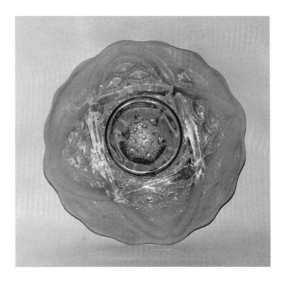

**Wishbone and Drape Plate
Blue Opalescent**

**Wreath and Shell Creamer
Blue Opalescent**

**Wreath and Shell Spooner
Blue Opalescent**

	Blue	Green	White	Vaseline Canary	Cranberry	Other
Abalone						
Bowl novelties	30.00		24.00	30.00		
Adonis Pineapple						
Claret bottle	300.00*					350.00* Amber
Acorn Burrs						
(& Bark)						
Bowl, master	100.00		80.00			
Bowl, sauce	40.00		30.00			
Alaska						
Pitcher	385.00		320.00	370.00		375.00 Emerald
Tumbler	70.00		56.00	65.00		70.00 Emerald
Covered Butter	370.00		255.00	375.00		275.00 Emerald
Sugar w/lid	160.00		125.00	135.00		140.00 Emerald
Creamer	75.00		55.00	65.00		70.00 Emerald
Spooner	75.00		55.00	65.00		70.00 Emerald
Bowl, master	160.00		135.00	150.00		150.00 Emerald
Bowl, sauce	55.00		20.00	45.00		40.00 Emerald
Cruet	275.00		245.00	260.00		270.00 Emerald
Tray	180.00		130.00	150.00		160.00 Emerald
Banana Boat	265.00		245.00	260.00		260.00 Emerald
Shakers, pair	100.00		65.00	90.00		75.00 Emerald
Bride's Basket	250.00		125.00			
Arabian Nights						
Pitcher	275.00		210.00	265.00	895.00	
Tumbler	60.00		40.00	67.00	100.00	
Syrup	220.00		185.00	225.00		
Argonaut Shell						
(Nautilus)*						
Pitcher	475.00		340.00			
Tumbler	100.00		70.00	125.00		
Butter	295.00		235.00			
Sugar	225.00		195.00			
Creamer	190.00		140.00			
Spooner	190.00		125.00			
Bowl, Master	100.00		80.00			
Bowl, Sauce	45.00		40.00			
Cruet	450.00		200.00			
Shakers, pair	90.00		70.00	110.00		
Jelly Compote	85.00		60.00	85.00		
Novety Bowls	50.00		30.00			
Ascot (English)						
Bowl	50.00					
Creamer	65.00			65.00		
Astro						
Bowl 8"	48.00	45.00	35.00	40.00		

	Blue	Green	White	Vaseline Canary	Cranberry	Other
Aurora Borealis						
Novelty Vase	55.00	65.00	35.00			
Autumn Leaves						
Bowl	40.00		30.00			
Banana Bowl	45.00		30.00			
Baby Coinspot*						
Syrup			95.00			
Barbells						
Bowl	38.00	42.00	26.00	40.00		
Basketweave Base*						
Console Set 3 pcs.	225.00		185.00			
Nappy (various)	40.00	35.00	28.00	37.00		
Beaded Ovals & Holly						
Spooner	70.00*		50.00*	75.00*		
Beaded Ovals in Sand						
Pitcher	390.00	380.00				
Tumbler	80.00	70.00				
Butter	270.00	255.00				
Sugar	225.00	220.00				
Creamer	80.00	70.00				
Spooner	80.00	70.00				
Bowl, Master	70.00	65.00				
Bowl, Sauce	25.00	20.00				
Cruet	220.00	200.00				
Shakers, pair	90.00	80.00				
Toothpick Holder	185.00	180.00				
Nappy	38.00	35.00				
Beaded Cable						
Bowl, Footed	40.00	32.00	25.00	35.00		
Rosebowl, Footed	45.00	38.00	40.00	40.00		
Beaded Drapes						
Bowl, Footed	38.00	35.00	32.00	40.00		
Banana Bowl, Footed	40.00	37.00	34.00	42.00		
Beaded Fan						
Bowl, Footed	37.00	42.00	30.00			
Rosebowl, Footed	40.00	45.00	35.00			
Beaded Fleur De Lis						
Compote (var. tops)	45.00	45.00	35.00			

	Blue	Green	White	Vaseline Canary	Cranberry	Other
Beaded Star Medallion						
Shade		48.00	40.00			
Beaded Stars						
Plate (add 15% adv.)	75.00					
Bowl	40.00	45.00	30.00			
Rosebowl	50.00	48.00	32.00			
Beaded Moon & Stars						
Bowl	60.00*					
Beads & Bark						
Vase, footed	60.00	55.00		60.00		
Beads & Curleycues						
Novelty Shapes, ftd.	42.00	37.00	30.00			
(Beatty) Honeycomb*						
Pitcher	175.00		130.00			
Tumbler	50.00		35.00			
Butter	190.00		150.00			
Sugar	90.00		70.00			
Creamer	50.00		40.00			
Spooner	50.00		40.00			
Bowl, Master	45.00		35.00			
Bowl, Sauce	28.00		18.00			
Cruet	185.00		150.00			
Toothpick Holder	240.00		200.00			
Celery Vase	78.00		70.00			
Shakers, pair	70.00		50.00			
Mustard Pot	90.00		70.00			
Mug	48.00		32.00			
Individual cream/sugar set	140.00*		115.00*			
Beatty Rib						
Pitcher	170.00		125.00			
Tumbler	45.00		30.00			
Butter	180.00		90.00			
Sugar	125.00		70.00			
Creamer	50.00		25.00			
Spooner	50.00		25.00			
Bowl, Master	40.00		20.00			
Bowl, Sauce	20.00		15.00			
Celery Vase	75.00		60.00			
Mug	45.00		30.00			
Ashtray, Cigar	75.00*					
Mustard Jar	140.00		100.00			
Nappy (Various)	30.00		20.00			
Shakers, pair	65.00		50.00			
Salt dip	50.00		35.00			
Cracker Jar	110.00		85.00			

	Blue	Green	White	Vaseline Canary	Cranberry	Other
Beatty Rib (Continued)						
Sugar Shaker	100.00		90.00			
Finger Bowl	28.00		20.00			
Match Holder	45.00		30.00			
Toothpick	50.00		28.00			
Beatty Swirl						
Pitcher	175.00		110.00	170.00		
Tumbler	30.00		30.00	45.00		
Butter	160.00		140.00			
Sugar	125.00		70.00			
Creamer	65.00		50.00			
Spooner	65.00		50.00			
Bowl, Master	45.00		38.00			
Bowl, Sauce	25.00		17.00			
Celery Vase	75.00		60.00			
Mug	50.00		35.00	70.00		
Syrup	210.00		180.00	225.00		
Water Tray	80.00		60.00	85.00		
Berry Patch						
Nappy (dome base)	45.00	40.00	30.00			
Blackberry						
Nappy	35.00	30.00	25.00			
Blocked Thumbprint & Beads						
Nappy	35.00	35.00	25.00			
Blooms & Blossoms						
Nappy, Handled	47.00	45.00	35.00			
Blossom & Palms						
Bowl	42.00	40.00	30.00			
Blossom & Web						
Bowl	65.00	60.00	35.00			
Blown Drape						
Pitcher	165.00	150.00	135.00		160.00	
Tumbler	50.00	40.00	25.00		38.00	
Barber Bottle	110.00	105.00	80.00		100.00	
(Blown) Twist						
Pitcher	250.00	240.00	200.00	245.00	875.00	
Tumbler	50.00	45.00	35.00	40.00	100.00	
Sugar Shaker	85.00	75.00	60.00	80.00	380.00	
Syrup	175.00		155.00		295.00*	
Boggy Bayou						
Vase	34.00	30.00	20.00			45.00 Amethyst

	Blue	Green	White	Vaseline Canary	Cranberry	Other
Brideshead (English)						
Butter	75.00					
Sugar	60.00					
Creamer	57.00					
Celery Vase	50.00					
Bowl Novelties	45.00					
Broken Pillar						
Compote	45.00			40.00		
(Bubble) Lattice						
Pitcher, Var. (Avg.)	250.00	240.00	200.00	265.00	725.00	
Tumbler, Var. (Avg.)	40.00	40.00	30.00	45.00	95.00	
Butter	180.00	175.00	140.00	190.00	685.00	
Sugar	90.00	85.00	65.00	95.00	390.00	
Creamer	40.00	35.00	30.00	47.00	140.00	
Spooner	50.00	35.00	30.00	47.00	195.00	
Bowl, Master	60.00	55.00	35.00	60.00	50.00	
Sauce	25.00	20.00	16.00	27.00	25.00	
Cruet	150.00	150.00	110.00	160.00	145.00	
Syrup	160.00	165.00	127.00	175.00	600.00	
Sugar Shaker	180.00	167.00	110.00	150.00	280.00	
Toothpick holder	260.00	240.00	120.00	265.00	250.00-450.00	
(Various prices averaged)						
Bride's Basket	65.00	60.00	40.00	70.00	120.00	
Fingerbowl	35.00	30.00	20.00	35.00	90.00	
Shakers, Various	100.00	95.00	80.00	115.00	210.00	
Celery Vase					100.00	
Bulbous Base Coinspot						
Sugar Shaker	100.00		80.00		130.00	
Bullseye						
Bowl	40.00				45.00	
Water Bottle			150.00		225.00	
Shade	60.00		40.00			
Bushel Basket*						
Novelty, Ftd.	100.00		90.00			
Button Panels						
Bowl	40.00		30.00	45.00		
Rosebowl	42.00		35.00	50.00		
Buttons & Braids						
Pitcher	175.00	145.00	125.00		395.00	
Tumbler	40.00	45.00	30.00		85.00	
Bowl	45.00	50.00	35.00		80.00	
Cabbage Leaf						
Novelty, Ftd.	80.00	60.00	45.00			

	Blue	Green	White	Vaseline Canary	Cranberry	Other
Calyx						
Vase	55.00		40.00	60.00		
Carousel						
Bowl	50.00	45.00	35.00			
Cashews						
Bowl	40.00	40.00	22.00			
Cherry Panels						
Bowl Novelties, Ftd.	75.00		60.00	70.00		
Chippendale (English)						
Compote	50.00			60.00		
Basket	40.00			37.00		
Christmas Pearls						
Cruet	265.00	250.00				
Shakers, Pair	95.00	90.00				
Christmas Snowflake						
Pitcher (2 types)	600.00		485.00		900.00	
Tumbler	85.00		70.00		100.00	
Chrysanthemum Base Swirl						
Pitcher	375.00		335.00		800.00	
Tumbler	80.00		60.00		100.00	
Butter	300.00		270.00		500.00	
Sugar	180.00		170.00		350.00	
Creamer	80.00		65.00		395.00	
Spooner	80.00		65.00		195.00	
Bowl, Master	48.00		40.00		100.00	
Bowl, Sauce	30.00		25.00		38.00	
Cruet	200.00		160.00		450.00	
Syrup	185.00		160.00		465.00	
Sugar Shaker	190.00		170.00		250.00	
Toothpick Holder	85.00		65.00		295.00	
Shakers, Pair	120.00		90.00		125.00	
Finger Bowl	35.00		30.00		60.00	
Celery Vase	125.00		100.00		195.00	
Straw Holder w/lid	450.00		390.00		1,000.00*	
Mustard Pot	140.00		110.00		190.00	
Chicks w/Leaf and Scroll						
Plate 7"	100.00					
Circle Scroll						
Pitcher	450.00	400.00	400.00			
Tumbler	90.00	85.00	70.00			
Butter	450.00	310.00	275.00			
Sugar	225.00	210.00	200.00			

	Blue	Green	White	Vaseline Canary	Cranberry	Other	
Circle Scroll(Continued)							
Creamer	65.00	60.00	25.00				
Spooner	125.00	130.00	50.00				
Bowl, Master	125.00	115.00	100.00				
Bowl, Sauce	40.00	37.00	30.00				
Cruet	365.00	350.00	325.00				
Shakers, Pair	285.00	260.00	135.00				
Jelly Compote	145.00	135.00	100.00				
Coinspot* (includes variants— prices averaged)							
Pitcher	225.00	130.00	90.00	150.00	360.00	170.00	Rubina
Tumbler	40.00	40.00	30.00	36.00	70.00	60.00	Rubina
Bowl, Master	45.00	40.00	30.00		60.00		
Bowl, Sauce	28.00	26.00	16.00		35.00		
Syrup	160.00	165.00	135.00		370.00	285.00	Rubina
Cruet (Various)	240.00	240.00	100.00	230.00	350.00	360.00	Rubina
Shakers, each	130.00	95.00	70.00	90.00	160.00		
Compote	50.00	45.00	35.00				
Sugar Shaker	90.00	95.00	75.00	90.00	350.00	225.00	Rubina
Novelty Bowls	60.00	55.00	40.00		65.00		
Celery Vase	125.00	110.00	70.00	115.00	160.00		
Tumble-up	140.00		120.00		260.00		
Toothpick Holder	250.00	240.00	100.00	225.00	260.00	265.00	Rubina
Barber Bottle					275.00		
Cleopatra's Fan							
Vase	50.00*	60.00*					
Colonial Stairsteps							
Creamer	90.00						
Sugar	90.00						
Toothpick Holder	175.00						
Consolidated Crisscross							
Pitcher			500.00		900.00		
Tumbler			90.00		110.00		
Sugar			300.00		350.00		
Butter			400.00		700.00		
Creamer			210.00		350.00		
Spooner			205.00		265.00		
Bowl, Master			100.00		165.00		
Bowl, Sauce			45.00		55.00		
Shakers, each			75.00		95.00	150.00	Rubina
Cruet			250.00		750.00		
Sugar Shaker			290.00		500.00	600.00	Rubina
Syrup			320.00		795.00	675.00	Rubina
Finger Bowl			80.00		100.00		
Celery Vase			120.00		165.00		
Mustard Pot			145.00		185.00		
Toothpick Holder			175.00		475.00		
Ivy Ball			280.00*		650.00		

	Blue	Green	White	Vaseline Canary	Cranberry	Other	
Contessa (English)							
Basket, Handled	55.00					65.00	Amber
Pitcher	110.00					120.00*	Amber
Breakfast Set Ftd.	125.00*					130.00*	Amber
(2 pieces)							
Coral							
Bowl	40.00	38.00	28.00	35.00			
Corn Vase*							
Fancy Vase	195.00	250.00	90.00	130.00			
Cornucopia							
Handled Basket	50.00		30.00				
Coronation (English)							
Pitcher	185.00			175.00			
Tumbler	35.00			30.00			
Crown Jewels (English)							
Pitcher	175.00						
Tumbler	50.00						
Curtain Call							
Caster Set – rare						450.00	Cobalt
Daffodils							
Pitcher	200.00	235.00	170.00	200.00	280.00		
Tumbler – rare	350.00	265.00	130.00	350.00	475.00		
Oil Lamp	250.00	225.00	180.00	210.00	250.00		
Dahlia Twist							
Vase	50.00	40.00	25.00				
Epergne	125.00	115.00	90.00				
Daisy Block (English)							
Rowboat, 4 sizes		75.00*	60.00*				
Daisy & Button (English)							
Lifeboat				60.00			
Daisy May (Leaf Rays)							
Bon-Bon	30.00	30.00	16.00				
Daisy & Fern*							
Pitcher (3 shapes)	275.00	265.00	185.00		200.00-600.00		
Tumbler	40.00	50.00	26.00		80.00		
Butter	200.00	210.00	160.00		250.00		
Sugar	95.00	110.00	65.00		225.00		
Creamer	65.00	70.00	40.00		395.00		
Vase	125.00	120.00	70.00		175.00		
Spooner	65.00	70.00	40.00		350.00		

	Blue	Green	White	Vaseline Canary	Cranberry	Other	
Daisy & Fern* (Continued)							
Bowl, Master	70.00	85.00	45.00		110.00		
Bowl, Sauce	30.00	35.00	20.00		42.00		
Sugar shaker	175.00	190.00	145.00		240.00		
Syrup, Various	160.00-215.00	170.00-200.00	95.00-180.00		220.00-500.00		
Toothpick Holder	140.00	150.00	100.00		175.00		
Shakers, pair	290.00	200.00	150.00		265.00		
Mustard Pot	85.00	95.00	70.00		135.00		
Cruet	180.00	160.00	125.00		485.00		
Perfume Bottle	150.00	170.00	100.00		240.00		
Night Lamp	190.00	210.00	140.00		285.00		
Pickle Castor	285.00	295.00	200.00		375.00		
Barber Bottle					350.00		
Rosebowl					95.00		
Daisy & Plume							
Bowl, Ftd.	45.00	40.00	35.00				
Daisy Dear							
Bowl	45.00	38.00	30.00				
Daisy In Crisscross							
Pitcher	295.00				425.00		
Tumbler	55.00				90.00		
Syrup	245.00				450.00		
Desert Garden							
Bowl	40.00	30.00	20.00				
Diamond & Oval Thumbprint							
Vase	30.00	35.00	20.00				
Diamond Point							
Vase	35.00	40.00	25.00				
Diamond Wave							
Pitcher w/Lid					140.00		
Tumbler					30.00		
Diamond Stem							
Vase	45.00						
Diamond Point & Fleur De Lis							
Bowl Novelty	45.00	50.00	37.00				
Diamond & Daisy							
Novelty Bowl (Goofus)			70.00				
Diamond Spearhead							
Pitcher	320.00	325.00	275.00	320.00		450.00	Cobalt
Tumbler	40.00	40.00	35.00	45.00		60.00	Cobalt
Goblet	95.00	90.00	70.00	95.00		110.00	Cobalt

	Blue	Green	White	Vaseline Canary	Cranberry	Other	
Diamond Spearhead (Continued)							
Butter	250.00	270.00	175.00	200.00		220.00	Cobalt
Sugar	140.00	135.00	110.00	140.00		175.00	Cobalt
Creamer	90.00	95.00	70.00	90.00		125.00	Cobalt
Spooner	125.00	100.00	60.00	125.00		95.00	Cobalt
Bowl, Master	60.00	60.00	40.00	60.00			
Bowl, Sauce	30.00	30.00	20.00	25.00			
Toothpick Holder				160.00		220.00	Cobalt
Mug	45.00	50.00	30.00	45.00		70.00	Cobalt
						55.00	Emerald
Syrup	300.00	350.00	260.00	300.00		650.00	Cobalt
Celery Vase	110.00	115.00	90.00	115.00		175.00	Cobalt
Shakers, Pair	80.00	90.00	60.00	85.00		130.00	Cobalt
Jelly Compote	95.00			100.00		160.00	Cobalt
Cup & Saucer Set				80.00		125.00	Cobalt
Tall Compote	120.00	125.00		120.00		185.00	Cobalt
Tall Creamer				115.00		140.00	Cobalt
Diamond Stem							
Vase			35.00	45.00			
Diamonds							
Pitcher (2 shapes)					375.00	200.00	Rubina
Vase (6" decorated)			25.00				
Cruet					295.00		
Dolly Madison							
Pitcher	350.00	360.00	295.00				
Tumbler	75.00	80.00	55.00				
Butter	300.00	320.00	265.00				
Sugar	125.00	135.00	90.00				
Creamer	80.00	90.00	65.00				
Spooner	70.00	75.00	55.00				
Bowl, Master	50.00	60.00	40.00				
Bowl, Sauce	25.00	30.00	20.00				
Dolphin & Herons							
Footed Novelty	75.00		60.00	85.00			
Dolphin*							
Compote	55.00		30.00	50.00			
Dolphin Petticoat							
Candlestick, pair	150.00		100.00	120.00			
Double Greek Key							
Pitcher	295.00		240.00				
Tumbler	65.00		40.00				
Butter	255.00		210.00				
Sugar	155.00		130.00				
Creamer	70.00		60.00				
Spooner	75.00		65.00				

	Blue	Green	White	Vaseline Canary	Cranberry	Other
Double Greek Key (Continued)						
Bowl, Master	60.00		50.00			
Bowl, Sauce	30.00		20.00			
Celery Vase	120.00		100.00			
Pickle Tray	110.00		80.00			
Shakers, pair	185.00		150.00			
Mustard Pot	170.00		135.00			
Toothpick Holder	185.00		160.00			
Dragon Lady						
Rosebowl	38.00	35.00	26.00			
Novelty Bowl	35.00	30.00	22.00			
Vase	40.00	37.00	28.00			
Drapery, Northwood's						
Pitcher	175.00		150.00			
Tumbler	35.00		18.00			
Butter	175.00		155.00			
Sugar	110.00		90.00			
Creamer	65.00		55.00			
Spooner	75.00		60.00			
Bowl, Master	110.00		80.00			
Bowl, Sauce	40.00		25.00	30.00		
Rosebowl	95.00		70.00			
Duchess (English)						
Pitcher	160.00		120.00	150.00		
Tumbler	20.00		18.00	25.00		
Butter	150.00		130.00	160.00		
Sugar	100.00		80.00	100.00		
Creamer	50.00		40.00	55.00		
Spooner	60.00		50.00	65.00		
Bowl, Master	90.00		60.00	75.00		
Bowl, Sauce	25.00		15.00	28.00		
Toothpick Holder	140.00		110.00	150.00		
Cruet	180.00		140.00	190.00		
Lampshade	85.00		70.00			
Elipse & Diamond						
Pitcher					375.00	
Tumbler					90.00*	
English Spool						
Vase				55.00		
Everglades						
Pitcher	430.00		300.00	375.00		
Tumbler	70.00		45.00	70.00		
Butter	230.00		200.00	280.00		
Sugar	135.00		100.00	125.00		
Creamer	125.00		70.00	90.00		
Spooner	90.00		75.00	90.00		

	Blue	Green	White	Vaseline Canary	Cranberry	Other
Everglades (Continued)						
Oval Bowl, Master	125.00		100.00	135.00		
Oval Bowl, Sauce	40.00		25.00	30.00		
Cruet	450.00		300.00	300.00		
Shakers, pair	230.00		200.00	220.00		
Jelly Compote	90.00	125.00	75.00	115.00		
Fan						
Pitcher	275.00	260.00	200.00			
Tumbler	30.00	27.00	18.00			
Butter	350.00	340.00	200.00			
Sugar	175.00	160.00	140.00			
Creamer	75.00	60.00	50.00			
Spooner	75.00	60.00	50.00			
Bowl, Master	60.00	55.00	38.00			
Bowl, Sauce	28.00	25.00	16.00			
Gravy Boat	40.00	35.00	25.00			
Novelty Bowls	35.00	32.00	20.00			
Fancy Fantails						
Rosebowl	40.00	35.00	20.00	40.00		
Novelty Bowl	35.00	30.00	16.00	35.00		
Feathers						
Vase	28.00	26.00	18.00			
Fenton Drapery						
Pitcher	400.00*	390.00*	280.00*			
Tumbler	60.00*	55.00*	37.00*			
Fern						
Pitcher, Various	225.00		160.00		750.00	
Tumbler	40.00		30.00		90.00	
Butter	240.00		210.00		360.00	
Sugar	180.00		160.00		195.00	
Bowl, Master	90.00		70.00		120.00	
Bowl, Sauce	40.00		25.00		55.00	
Sugar Shaker, Var.	90.00		70.00		500.00	
Syrup	265.00		140.00		190.00	
Cruet	190.00		145.00		425.00*	
Shakers, pair	150.00		90.00		120.00	
Celery Vase	100.00		85.00		130.00	
Mustard Pot	130.00		110.00		145.00	
Toothpick Holder (rare)	300.00		170.00		450.00	
Finger Bowl	55.00		40.00		90.00	
Barber Bottle	120.00		90.00		240.00	
Creamer	110.00		85.00		135.00	
Spooner	110.00		85.00		125.00	
Finecut & Roses						
Novelty Bowls	40.00	45.00	30.00			

	Blue	Green	White	Vaseline Canary	Cranberry	Other
Fishnet						
Epergne			110.00			160.00 Emerald
Fish In The Sea						
Vase	75.00	70.00	55.00			
Fishscale & Beads						
Novelty Bowl	35.00		22.00			
Flora						
Pitcher	475.00		400.00	460.00		
Tumbler	75.00		55.00	70.00		
Butter	250.00		160.00	185.00		
Sugar	120.00		100.00	115.00		
Creamer	90.00		70.00	80.00		
Spooner	90.00		80.00	90.00		
Bowl, Master	100.00		75.00	95.00		
Bowl, Sauce	45.00		20.00	35.00		
Cruet	650.00		400.00	585.00		
Toothpick Holder	400.00		240.00	310.00		
Syrup	350.00		260.00	325.00		
Shakers, pair	350.00		250.00	320.00		
Jelly Compote	140.00		90.00	115.00		
Celery Vase	115.00		70.00	95.00		
Bowl Novelties	50.00		35.00	45.00		
Floral Eyelet						
Pitcher – rare	450.00*					
Fluted Bars & Beads						
Rosebowl	40.00	35.00	30.00			
Novelty Bowls	45.00	40.00	35.00			
Vase Novelty	50.00	45.00	40.00			
Fluted Scrolls With Vine						
Vase, Footed	45.00		30.00	50.00		
Fruit Patch						
Compote	75.00			65.00		
Fluted Scrolls						
Pitcher	200.00		140.00	195.00		
Tumbler	85.00		30.00	50.00		
Butter	160.00		140.00	170.00		
Sugar	125.00		80.00	90.00		
Spooner	50.00		40.00	50.00		
Creamer	60.00		40.00	60.00		
Bowl, Master	70.00		45.00	65.00		
Bowl, Sauce	25.00		15.00	20.00		
Cruet	180.00		160.00	175.00		
Shakers, Pair	80.00		60.00	75.00		
Epergne, Small	110.00		80.00	125.00		

	Blue	Green	White	Vaseline Canary	Cranberry	Other	
Fluted Scrolls (Continued)							
Rosebowl	125.00		75.00	110.00			
Bowl Novelties	40.00		30.00	40.00			
Puff Box	55.00		40.00	50.00			
Frosted Leaf & Basketweave							
Butter	260.00			240.00			
Sugar	170.00			150.00			
Creamer	140.00			125.00			
Spooner	130.00			90.00			
Gonterman (Adonis) Hob							
Cruet						350.00	Amber
Gonterman (Adonis) Swirl							
Pitcher	350.00					395.00	Amber
Tumbler	70.00					75.00	Amber
Butter	300.00					325.00	Amber
Sugar	200.00					210.00	Amber
Creamer	80.00					90.00	Amber
Spooner	80.00					90.00	Amber
Bowl, Master	75.00					85.00	Amber
Bowl, Sauce	40.00					50.00	Amber
Cruet	300.00					320.00	Amber
Celery Vase	185.00					185.00	Amber
Syrup	350.00					365.00	Amber
Shade	85.00					110.00	Amber
Toothpick Holder	200.00					150.00	Amber
Grape & Cable							
Centerpiece Bowl			110.00				
Bon-Bon				140.00*			
Grape & Cherry							
Bowl	50.00		45.00				
Grapevine Cluster							
Vase, Footed	65.00		40.00				
Greek Key & Ribs							
Bowl Novelty	55.00	40.00	30.00				
Greek Key & Scales							
Bowl Novelty	50.00	50.00	30.00				
Heart-Handle Open O's							
Ring Tray	85.00	75.00	50.00				
Hearts & Clubs							
Bowl, Footed	45.00	40.00	28.00				
Hearts & Flowers							
Compote	75.00		55.00				
Bowl	60.00		35.00				

	Blue	Green	White	Vaseline Canary	Cranberry	Other	
Heatherbloom							
Vase	30.00	28.00	18.00				
Herringbone							
Pitcher	500.00		425.00		695.00		
Tumbler	90.00		57.00		135.00		
Cruet	265.00		200.00		665.00		
Hilltop Vines							
Novelty Chalice	65.00	57.00	38.00				
Hobnail & Panelled Thumbprint							
Pitcher	300.00		150.00	275.00			
Tumbler	70.00		45.00	65.00			
Butter	180.00		140.00	170.00			
Sugar	110.00		90.00	85.00			
Creamer	70.00		60.00	65.00			
Spooner	80.00		65.00	70.00			
Bowl, Master	70.00		60.00	65.00			
Bowl, Sauce	35.00		26.00	32.00			
Hobnail 4-Footed							
Butter			150.00	190.00		210.00	Cobalt
Sugar			80.00	120.00		135.00	Cobalt
Creamer			60.00	70.00		85.00	Cobalt
Spooner			65.00	75.00		90.00	Cobalt
Hobnail, Hobbs							
Pitcher (5 Sizes)	200.00-320.00		130.00-220.00	200.00-275.00	350.00-500.00	250.00-350.00	Rubina
Tumbler	70.00		50.00	70.00	85.00	100.00	Rubina
Butter	250.00		180.00	245.00	290.00		
Sugar	170.00		130.00	165.00	195.00		
Creamer	100.00		100.00	95.00	150.00		
Spooner	90.00		90.00	95.00	150.00		
Bowl, Master (Square)	90.00		70.00	95.00	140.00		
Bowl, Sauce (Square)	35.00		20.00	30.00	50.00		
Cruet	190.00		170.00	190.00	395.00		
Syrup	215.00		180.00	210.00	350.00	325.00	Rubina
Finger Bowl	60.00		45.00	55.00	90.00		
Barber Bottle	140.00		100.00	130.00	180.00	225.00	Rubina
Celery Vase	160.00		90.00	100.00			
Water Tray	160.00		110.00	140.00			
Bride's Basket	425.00			400.00	490.00	500.00	Rubina
Lemonade Set, Complete	600.00				650.00		
Hobnail In Square* (Vesta)							
Pitcher			200.00				
Tumbler			30.00				
Butter			180.00				
Sugar			120.00				

	Blue	Green	White	Vaseline Canary	Cranberry	Other
Hobnail In Square* (Vesta) (Continued)						
Creamer			70.00			
Spooner			75.00			
Bowl, Master			60.00			
Bowl, Sauce			20.00			
Celery Vase			120.00			
Shakers, pair			85.00			
Compote (Various)			70.00-90.00			
Barber Bottle			100.00			
Hobnail, Northwood's						
Pitcher			90.00			
Tumbler			20.00			
Butter			125.00			
Sugar			95.00			
Creamer			45.00			
Spooner			45.00			
Bowl, Master			50.00			
Bowl, Sauce			20.00			
Mug			70.00			
Celery Vase			80.00			
Breakfast Set (2 piece set)			120.00			
Holly						
Bowl 10"			65.00			
Honeycomb						
Pitcher	200.00		150.00		395.00	350.00 Amber
Tumbler	50.00		30.00		55.00	70.00 Amber
Cracker Jar	265.00		200.00		285.00	350.00 Amber
Syrup	275.00		210.00		300.00	375.00 Amber
Barber Bottle	140.00		95.00		150.00	160.00 Amber
Honeycomb						
Vase	50.00*					
Honeycomb & Clover						
Pitcher	365.00	325.00	200.00			
Tumbler	90.00	75.00	55.00			
Butter	325.00	300.00	250.00			
Sugar	210.00	180.00	130.00			
Creamer	100.00	90.00	70.00			
Spooner	120.00	100.00	80.00			
Bowl, Master	60.00	50.00	40.00			
Bowl, Sauce	30.00	26.00	18.00			
Bowl Novelty	45.00	40.00	26.00			
Idyll						
Pitcher	350.00	340.00	290.00			
Tumbler	80.00	75.00	60.00			
Butter	325.00	365.00	285.00			
Sugar	95.00	160.00	80.00			

	Blue	Green	White	Vaseline Canary	Cranberry	Other
Idyll (Continued)						
Creamer	90.00	85.00	38.00			
Spooner	130.00	90.00	60.00			
Bowl, Master	45.00	50.00	30.00			
Bowl, Sauce 4x6"	28.00-32.00	28.00	18.00			
Toothpick Holder	350.00	280.00	210.00			
Cruet	185.00	190.00	160.00			
Shakers, pair	90.00	95.00	80.00			
Tray	90.00	85.00	75.00			
Interior Panel						
Fan Vase	40.00	40.00	20.00	40.00		55.00 Amethyst
						45.00 Amber
Inside Ribbing						
Bowl, Master	50.00		35.00	55.00		
Bowl, Sauce	24.00		16.00	25.00		
Butter	220.00		130.00	225.00		
Sugar	100.00		80.00	110.00		
Spooner	50.00		40.00	60.00		
Creamer	50.00		40.00	60.00		
Pitcher	250.00		135.00	235.00		
Tumbler	50.00		26.00	40.00		
Celery Vase	45.00		25.00	40.00		
Syrup	135.00		90.00	120.00		
Jelly Compote	40.00		20.00	35.00		
Toothpick Holder	190.00		145.00	180.00		
Cruet	120.00		85.00	115.00		
Shakers, pair	90.00		60.00	80.00		
Tray	45.00		30.00	45.00		
Rosebowl	70.00					
Intaglio						
Pitcher	200.00		115.00			
Tumbler	100.00		50.00			
Butter	450.00		200.00			
Sugar	135.00		85.00			
Creamer	60.00		25.00			
Spooner	65.00		35.00			
Bowl, Master, Ftd.	210.00		70.00			
Bowl, Sauce, Ftd.	20.00		15.00			
Shakers, pair	85.00		60.00			
Jelly Compote	40.00		30.00			
Novelty Bowl	45.00		30.00	50.00		
Cruet	175.00		125.00	285.00*		
Inverted Fan & Feather*						
Pitcher	750.00		550.00			
Tumbler	85.00		60.00			
Butter	400.00		320.00			
Sugar	280.00		190.00			
Creamer	140.00		100.00			

	Blue	Green	White	Vaseline Canary	Cranberry	Other
Inverted Fan & Feather* **(Continued)**						
Spooner	140.00		100.00			
Bowl, Master	295.00		200.00			
Bowl, Sauce	45.00		25.00			
Cruet, rare	395.00					
Shakers, pair, rare	250.00					
Jelly Compote rare	150.00		125.00			
Toothpick, rare	400.00					
Punchbowl, rare	450.00					
Punch Cup, rare	20.00					
Novelty Bowl, v. rare				240.00*		
Iris With Meander						
Pitcher	375.00	350.00	260.00	270.00		
Tumbler	75.00	70.00	55.00	60.00		
Butter	275.00	260.00	230.00	270.00		
Sugar	150.00	125.00	90.00	135.00		
Creamer	75.00	70.00	60.00	75.00		
Spooner	75.00	60.00	50.00	85.00		
Bowl, Master	195.00	80.00	60.00	85.00		
Bowl, Sauce, 2 Szs	30.00-40.00	25.00-30.00	18.00-22.00	26.00		
Toothpick Holder	125.00	85.00	45.00	80.00		
Shakers, pair	200.00	185.00	165.00	190.00		
Cruet	450.00	350.00	260.00	385.00		390.00 Amber
Jelly Compote	45.00	40.00	30.00	45.00		
Vase, Tall	50.00	45.00	40.00	60.00		
Pickle Dish	75.00	70.00	50.00	75.00		
Plate	135.00	132.00	110.00	130.00		
Jackson						
Pitcher	450.00		370.00	425.00		
Tumbler	75.00		60.00	80.00		
Butter	200.00		125.00	200.00		
Sugar	115.00		85.00	110.00		
Creamer	70.00		55.00	60.00		
Spooner	70.00		55.00	60.00		
Bowl, Master	80.00		60.00	75.00		
Bowl, Sauce	30.00		18.00	25.00		
Cruet	175.00		155.00	170.00		
Epergne, Small	150.00		82.00	100.00		
Candy Dish	45.00		30.00	40.00		
Powder Jar	55.00		30.00	50.00		
Jefferson Spool						
Vase	40.00	30.00	26.00			
Jefferson Shield						
Bowl	75.00*	75.00*	60.00*			
Jefferson Wheel						
Bowl	45.00	40.00	30.00			

	Blue	Green	White	Vaseline Canary	Cranberry	Other
Jewel & Fan						
Bowl	40.00	35.00	28.00			
Banana Bowl	90.00	110.00				
Jewel & Flower						
Pitcher	650.00		275.00	450.00		
Tumbler	80.00		55.00	70.00		
Butter	350.00		195.00	325.00		
Sugar	190.00		70.00	185.00		
Creamer	95.00		55.00	150.00		
Spooner	95.00		40.00	120.00		
Bowl, Master	60.00		40.00	60.00		
Bowl, Sauce	30.00		20.00	28.00		
Cruet	650.00		210.00	585.00		
Shakers, pair	140.00		95.00	130.00		
Novelty Bowl	35.00		26.00	35.00		
Jewelled Heart						
Pitcher	225.00	165.00	95.00			
Tumbler	80.00	55.00	25.00			
Butter	300.00	285.00	200.00			
Sugar	175.00	155.00	120.00			
Creamer	110.00	110.00	90.00			
Spooner	110.00	110.00	85.00			
Bowl, Master	52.00	50.00	40.00			
Bowl, Sauce	28.00	25.00	25.00			
Cruet	450.00	395.00	300.00			
Novelty Bowls	30.00	28.00	20.00			
Plate, Small	40.00	45.00	35.00			
Compote	125.00	120.00	85.00			
Toothpick	225.00	200.00	175.00			
Jewels & Drapery						
Novelty Bowl	40.00	35.00	25.00			
Vase (from bowl)	30.00	28.00	18.00			
Jolly Bear						
Bowl	110.00	100.00	80.00			
Lattice Medallions						
Bowl	45.00	40.00	30.00			
Lattice & Daisy						
Tumbler	70.00*		50.00*	60.00*		
Lady Caroline (English)						
Creamer	55.00					
Sugar	50.00					
Basket	58.00					
Laura (Single Flower Framed)						
Novelty Bowl	35.00	40.00	25.00			

	Blue	Green	White	Vaseline Canary	Cranberry	Other
Lady Chippendale (English)						
Compote, Tall						75.00* Cobalt
Leaf & Beads						
Novelty Bowls, Footed or Dome	45.00	40.00	30.00			
Leaf & Diamonds						
Novelty Bowl	38.00		28.00			
Leaf & Leaflets						
Novelty Bowl			30.00			
Leaf Chalice						
Novelty compote	90.00	85.00	40.00	65.00		
Leaf Mold						
Pitcher					495.00	
Tumbler					90.00	
Butter					385.00	
Sugar					265.00	
Creamer					115.00	
Spooner					110.00	
Bowl, Master					120.00	
Bowl, Sauce					40.00	
Syrup					350.00	
Sugar Shaker					320.00	
Celery Vase					300.00	
Shakers, pair					500.00	
Cruet					575.00	
Toothpick Holder					450.00	
Lined Heart						
Vase	35.00	32.00	25.00			
Little Nell						
Vase	30.00	26.00	15.00			
Lorna						
Vase	30.00		20.00	30.00		
Linking Rings (English)						
Novelty Bowl	50.00					
Pitcher	85.00					
Lords & Ladies						
Creamer	55.00					
Open Sugar	60.00					
Butter	85.00					
Little Swan (Pastel Swan)						
Novelty, 2 Sizes	85.00	70.00	50.00	75.00		

	Blue	Green	White	Vaseline Canary	Cranberry	Other
Lustre Flute						
Pitcher	325.00		270.00			
Tumbler	65.00		40.00			
Butter	285.00		125.00			
Sugar	175.00		90.00			
Creamer	90.00		55.00			
Spooner	90.00		55.00			
Bowl, Master	60.00		40.00			
Bowl, Sauce	25.00		20.00			
Custard Cup	28.00		16.00			
Vase	35.00		22.00			
Many Loops						
Bowl	40.00	30.00	25.00			
Many Ribs						
Vase	35.00		20.00	30.00		
Maple Leaf Chalice						
Novelty Shape	60.00	50.00	40.00	50.00		
Mary Ann						
Vase	60.00		35.00			
May Basket						
Basket Shape	35.00	30.00	20.00			
Meander						
Novelty Bowl	35.00	30.00	25.00			
Milky Way (Country Kitchen Variant)						
Bowl (rare Millersburg item)			150.00			
Miniature Epergne						
Novelty	125.00			115.00		
Maple Leaf						
Jelly Compote	60.00	55.00	40.00			
Netted Roses						
Bowl	60.00		36.00			
Northern Star						
Bowl	60.00	55.00	35.00			
Plate	90.00	85.00	55.00			
Banana Bowl	70.00	70.00	40.00			
Northwood Block						
Novelty Bowl	40.00	45.00	30.00	35.00		
Celery Vase	50.00	50.00	36.00	40.00		
Ocean Shell						
Novelty Footed	65.00	60.00	40.00			

	Blue	Green	White	Vaseline Canary	Cranberry	Other
Old Man Winter						
Basket, Small	55.00		30.00			
Basket, Large, Ftd.	65.00		35.00			
Opal Open* (Beaded Panels)						
Compote	30.00	35.00	22.00	28.00		
Rosebowl, Ftd.	38.00	42.00	26.00	32.00		
Open O's						
Ring Bowl, Handled	75.00	70.00	55.00	70.00		
Novelty Bowl	40.00	42.00	32.00	38.00		
Novelty Vase	35.00	37.00	26.00	32.00		
Opal Spiral						
Sugar	295.00*					
Tumbler	80.00*					
Over-Lapping Leaves (Leaf Tiers)						
Bowl, Footed	40.00	40.00	28.00			
Rosebowl, Footed	50.00	45.00	35.00			
Plate, Footed	60.00	57.00	42.00			
Over-All Hob						
Pitcher	190.00		150.00	175.00		
Tumbler	50.00		25.00	40.00		
Butter	210.00		160.00	200.00		
Sugar	130.00		90.00	125.00		
Creamer	50.00		40.00	45.00		
Spooner	60.00		45.00	55.00		
Bowl, Master	45.00		30.00	40.00		
Bowl, Sauce	20.00		16.00	18.00		
Toothpick Holder	18.00		135.00	175.00		
Celery Vase	65.00		45.00	60.00		
Finger Bowl	45.00		30.00	40.00		
Mug	65.00		45.00	70.00		
Palisades						
Vase Novelty	35.00	40.00	24.00	37.00		
Palm & Scroll						
Bowl, Footed	45.00	40.00	32.00			
Palm Beach						
Pitcher	385.00			350.00		
Tumbler	85.00			95.00		
Butter	275.00			260.00		
Sugar	120.00			180.00		
Creamer	75.00			120.00		
Spooner	110.00			125.00		
Bowl, Master	70.00			65.00		

	Blue	Green	White	Vaseline Canary	Cranberry	Other
Palm Beach (Continued)						
Bowl, Sauce, 2 Sizes	30.00			29.00		
Jelly Compote	120.00			175.00		
Nappy, Handled rare				350.00		
Plate 8" rare	395.00*			375.00		
Wine very rare				350.00		
Panelled Flowers						
Rosebowl, Ftd	55.00		30.00			
Nut Cup, Ftd.	60.00		35.00			
Panelled Holly						
Pitcher	500.00		300.00			
Tumbler	75.00		45.00			
Butter	300.00		220.00			
Sugar	225.00		110.00			
Creamer	125.00		50.00			
Spooner	125.00		60.00			
Bowl, Master	85.00		40.00			
Bowl, Sauce	35.00		20.00			
Shakers, pair	105.00		80.00			
Novelty Bowl	45.00		28.00			
Panelled Sprig*						
Cruet			115.00			
Toothpick Holder			70.00			
Shakers, pair			85.00			
Peacocks (On the Fence)						
Bowl	125.00		95.00			140.00 Cobalt
Pearl Flowers						
Nut Bowl, Footed	40.00	35.00	30.00			
Novelty Bowl, Footed	35.00	30.00	25.00			
Pearls & Scales						
Compote	55.00	50.00	20.00	65.00		
Piasa Bird						
Novelty Bowl	45.00		30.00			
Novelty Vase	55.00		40.00			
Picadilly (English)						
Basket, Small		60.00				
Plain Panels						
Vase	38.00	35.00	26.00			
Pinecones & Leaves						
Bowl			50.00			

	Blue	Green	White	Vaseline Canary	Cranberry	Other
Pineapple & Fan						
Vase				360.00		
Plain Jane						
Nappy, Footed	38.00					
Plume Panels (Variant)						
Vase – very rare		150.00				
Poinsettia						
Pitcher, either shape	275.00	195.00	120.00		850.00	
Tumbler	55.00	40.00	27.00		110.00	
Syrup, Various	325.00	275.00	200.00		350.00	
Sugar Shaker	250.00	200.00	140.00		300.00	
Fruit Bowl	70.00	65.00	40.00		90.00	
Poinsettia Lattice						
(Lattice & Poinsettia)						
Novelty Bowl	75.00		47.00	65.00		
Polka Dot*						
Pitcher, rare	190.00		100.00		795.00	
Tumbler	65.00		20.00		90.00*	
Syrup	200.00		95.00		600.00*	
Sugar Shaker	175.00		100.00		200.00	
Toothpick Holder	365.00		250.00		475.00	
Shakers, pair	60.00		40.00		270.00*	
Cruet	350.00*		200.00*		675.00*	
Popsickle Sticks						
Novelty Bowl, Ftd.	35.00	30.00	20.00			
Prince Albert & Victoria						
(English)						
Open Sugar	55.00			50.00		
Creamer, Footed	55.00			50.00		
Princess Diana (English)						
Crimped Plate	40.00			35.00		
Butter	90.00			85.00		
Open Sugar	60.00			55.00		
Creamer	50.00			50.00		
Pitcher	110.00			90.00		
Tumbler	35.00			35.00		
Water Tray	40.00			40.00		
Bisquit Set (Jar & Plate,						
Complete)	75.00			40.00		
Salad Bowl	40.00			70.00		
Novelty Bowl	40.00			45.00		
Compote, metal base	120.00*			35.00		

	Blue	Green	White	Vaseline Canary	Cranberry	Other
Prince William (English)						
Open Sugar	55.00			50.00		
Creamer	55.00			50.00		
Oval Plate	40.00			35.00		
Pitcher	90.00*			90.00*		
Tumbler	30.00*			28.00*		
Pulled Rib						
Novelty Bowl	30.00					
Vase	35.00					
Pump & Trough*						
Complete, 2 pieces	115.00		60.00	90.00		
Queen's Crown (English)						
Bowl, Small	30.00			25.00		
Compote, Low	45.00					
Quilted Pillow Sham (English)						
Oval Butter	90.00			80.00		
Creamer	60.00			55.00		
Question Mark						
Compote	50.00					
Rayed Heart						
Compote	55.00	55.00				
Reflecting Diamonds						
Novelty Bowl	40.00	36.00	22.00			
Reflections						
Novelty Bowl	35.00	30.00	18.00			
Regal (Northwoods)						
Pitcher	300.00	285.00	210.00			
Tumbler	60.00	55.00	40.00			
Butter	245.00	235.00	125.00			
Sugar	150.00	135.00	90.00			
Creamer	135.00	120.00	80.00			
Spooner	65.00	55.00	45.00			
Bowl, Master	65.00	55.00	30.00			
Bowl, Sauce	25.00	20.00	18.00			
Cruet	400.00	350.00	295.00			
Shakers, pair	90.00	80.00	70.00			
Celery Vase	165.00	140.00	90.00			
Reverse Drapery						
Novelty Bowl	28.00	26.00	15.00			
Plate	40.00	36.00	28.00			

	Blue	Green	White	Vaseline Canary	Cranberry	Other
Reverse Drapery (Continued)						
Vase	30.00	28.00	16.00			
Reverse Swirl						
Pitcher	195.00		140.00	185.00	750.00	
Tumbler	40.00		26.00	37.00	85.00	
Butter	190.00		135.00	165.00	240.00	
Sugar	175.00		100.00	150.00	210.00	
Creamer	150.00		90.00	120.00	175.00	
Spooner	95.00		70.00	90.00	130.00	
Bowl, Master	60.00		40.00	55.00	75.00	
Bowl, Sauce	25.00		16.00	20.00	35.00	
Cruet	245.00		100.00	140.00	450.00	
Toothpick Holder	130.00		90.00	120.00	245.00	
Sugar Shaker	135.00		110.00	135.00	245.00	
Syrup	150.00		90.00	135.00	395.00	
Mustard	70.00		40.00	65.00	95.00	
Water Bottle	140.00		92.00	130.00	180.00	
Finger Bowl	60.00		40.00		95.00	
Shakers, pair	85.00		55.00	80.00	150.00	
Custard Cup	45.00		28.00		140.00	
Mini-Lamp	350.00		180.00		290.00	
Celery Vase	150.00		95.00	145.00	190.00	
Cruet Set and Holder,						
4 pieces	275.00		200.00		350.00	
Oil Lamp					495.00	
Rib & Big Thumprints						
Vase	30.00	28.00	15.00			
Ribbed Opal Rings						
Pitcher rare					795.00	
Tumbler					100.00	
Ribbed Spiral						
Pitcher	480.00		350.00	450.00		
Tumbler	100.00		40.00	90.00		
Butter	350.00		260.00	325.00		
Sugar	175.00		125.00	165.00		
Creamer	60.00		40.00	55.00		
Spooner	70.00		42.00	60.00		
Bowl, Master	65.00		40.00	60.00		
Bowl, Sauce	26.00		18.00	24.00		
Plate	35.00		16.00	26.00		
Cup/Saucer,						
Complete	90.00		55.00	80.00		
Toothpick Holder	160.00		110.00	150.00		
Shakers, pair	195.00		110.00	185.00		
Jelly Compote	50.00		25.00	48.00		
Novelty Bowl	40.00		25.00	36.00		
Vase, Many Sizes	25.00-40.00		15.00-30.00	20.00-35.00		

	Blue	Green	White	Vaseline Canary	Cranberry	Other
Rippled Rib						
Vase			38.00			
Richelieu (English)						
Jelly Compote	65.00			60.00		
Novelty Bowl	60.00			55.00		
Creamer	58.00			52.00		
Divided Dish, rare	85.00			80.00		
Cracker Jar	180.00					
Handled Basket	75.00			65.00		
Ring Handle						
Shakers, Pair	90.00		60.00			
Ring Tray	95.00	85.00	58.00			

Note: I question these being the same pattern. The Ring tray looks like Opal Open (Beaded Panels)

	Blue	Green	White	Vaseline Canary	Cranberry	Other
Rose Show						
Bowl rare	140.00					
Roulette						
Novelty Bowl	38.00	32.00	25.00			
Ruffles & Rings ✓						
Rosebowl	45.00	48.00	36.00			
Nut Bowl	40.00	42.00	32.00			
Novelty Bowl	36.00	40.00	28.00			
Ribbed Coinspot						
Pitcher rare					1,000.00*	
Tumbler rare					160.00*	
Syrup rare					1,300.00*	
Celery Vase rare					250.00*	
Creamer rare					450.00*	
Sugar Shaker					495.00*	
Scheherezade						
Novelty Bowl	38.00	34.00	25.00			
Scroll With Acanthus						
Pitcher	375.00	360.00		350.00		
Tumbler	75.00	70.00		70.00		
Butter	350.00	320.00		340.00		
Sugar	150.00	135.00		125.00		
Creamer	60.00	45.00		70.00		
Spooner	65.00	57.00		50.00		
Bowl, Master	40.00	38.00		42.00		
Bowl, Sauce	20.00	20.00		24.00		
Jelly Compote	42.00	40.00		45.00		
Toothpick Holder	200.00	190.00		210.00		

	Blue	Green	White	Vaseline Canary	Cranberry	Other
Scroll With Acanthus (Continued)						
Shakers, pair	90.00	80.00		85.00		
Cruet	195.00	200.00		350.00		
Seaspray						
Nappy	37.00	32.00	22.00			
Seafoam						
Compote	50.00*		30.00*	45.00*		
Seaweed						
Pitcher	310.00		250.00		40.00	
Tumbler	55.00		30.00		110.00	
Butter	175.00		110.00		350.00	
Sugar	150.00		120.00		200.00	
Creamer	110.00		85.00		200.00	
Spooner	85.00		70.00		150.00	
Bowl, Master	45.00		35.00		100.00	
Bowl, Sauce	20.00		16.00		50.00	
Cruet (2 shapes)	235.00		100.00		450.00	
Syrup	150.00		115.00		175.00	
Sugar Shaker	190.00		160.00		350.00	
Toothpick Holder	295.00		220.00		450.00	
Celery Vase	150.00		115.00		225.00	
Shakers, pair	110.00		85.00		600.00*	
Barber Bottle (2 shapes)	150.00		105.00		295.00	
Mini-Lamp	425.00		375.00		1,700.00	
Pickle Castor, Complete					300.00	
Shell, Beaded						
Pitcher	500.00	560.00	475.00			
Tumbler	75.00	85.00	60.00			
Butter	450.00	470.00	400.00			
Sugar	185.00	195.00	160.00			
Creamer	75.00	90.00	60.00			
Spooner	95.00	85.00	60.00			
Bowl, Master	60.00	70.00	50.00			
Bowl, Sauce	28.00	32.00	25.00			
Cruet	350.00	395.00	340.00			
Toothpick Holder	400.00	500.00	390.00			
Shakers, pair	120.00	135.00	90.00			
Shell and Dots						
Rosebowl	35.00		20.00			
Shell & Wild Rose						
Novelty, Open-edge	40.00	35.00	28.00			
Simple Simon (Graceful)						
Compote		35.00	27.00			

	Blue	Green	White	Vaseline Canary	Cranberry	Other
Sir Lancelot (English)						
Novelty, Footed	57.00	50.00	35.00			
Somerset (English)						
Pitcher (Juice) 5½"	50.00			45.00		
Tumbler 3"	25.00			22.00		
Oval Dish 9"	37.00			35.00		
Square Dish	40.00			37.00		
Spanish Lace						
Pitcher, 3 Types	200.00-400.00		90.00-150.00	195.00-300.00	600.00-900.00	
Tumbler	50.00		30.00	60.00	100.00	
Butter	395.00		200.00	375.00	495.00	
Sugar	250.00		170.00	245.00	295.00	
Spooner	120.00		50.00	125.00	160.00	
Creamer	80.00		50.00	90.00	185.00	
Bowl, Master	75.00		40.00	80.00	140.00	
Bowl, Sauce	22.00		15.00	25.00	35.00	
Syrup	230.00		165.00	325.00	600.00	
Sugar Shaker	140.00		95.00	135.00	180.00	
Celery Vase	100.00		70.00	120.00	160.00	
Shakers, pair	100.00		60.00	100.00	200.00	
Finger Bowl	60.00		40.00	70.00	140.00	
Brides Basket 2 Sizes	105.00		70.00	110.00	160.00	
Jam Jar	260.00		170.00	275.00	450.00	
Cracker Jar (metal trim)	625.00				875.00	
Perfume Bottle	175.00		90.00	190.00	250.00	
Mini-Lamp	180.00		120.00	185.00	295.00	
Water Bottle	285.00		175.00	295.00	395.00	
Vase, Many Sizes	85.00		40.00	90.00	185.00	
Rosebowl, Several Sizes	50.00		40.00	45.00	90.00	
Cruet	230.00		170.00	240.00	650.00	
Liqueur Jug					750.00	
Spokes & Wheels						
Novelty Bowls	40.00	37.00	25.00			
Novelty Plate – rare	50.00	46.00				100.00 Aqua
Spool						
Compote	32.00	36.00	17.00			
Squirrel & Acorn						
Vase	75.00	60.00				
Bowl	70.00	55.00				
Stars & Stripes*						
Pitcher			210.00*		975.00	
Tumbler			60.00*		190.00	
Lamp Shade			50.00*		160.00	

	Blue	Green	White	Vaseline Canary	Cranberry	Other
Stars & Stripes* (Continued)						
Barber Bottle			90.00*		265.00*	
Stork & Rushes						
Mug rare	75.00					
Strawberry						
Bon Bon				200.00*		
Stripe*						
Pitcher	250.00		140.00	220.00	500.00	
Tumbler	45.00		28.00	55.00	75.00	
Syrup	250.00		160.00	225.00	280.00	
Toothpick Holder	225.00		170.00	240.00	300.00	
Condiment Set	350.00		160.00	340.00	400.00	
Barber Bottle	140.00		90.00	150.00	275.00	
Shakers, pair	85.00		60.00	95.00	125.00	
Rosebowl	65.00		40.00	70.00	100.00	
Oil Lamp					500.00	
Stripe, Wide						
Pitcher	200.00		140.00		400.00	
Tumbler	40.00		30.00		80.00	
Syrup	190.00		160.00		250.00	
Sugar Shaker	150.00		135.00		190.00	
Cruet	160.00		140.00		475.00	
Toothpick Holder	240.00	350.00	200.00		30.00	
Stag & Holly						
Bowl, Footed						500.00*Amethyst
Sunburst On Shield						
Pitcher	500.00			650.00*		
Tumbler	100.00			250.00*		
Bowl, Master	60.00		38.00	65.00		
Bowl, Sauce	22.00		16.00	24.00		
Breakfast Set,						
2 pieces	150.00		90.00	160.00		
Nappy rare	120.00		80.00	260.00*		
Cruet rare	255.00		160.00	675.00		
Butter	350.00		200.00	325.00		
Sugar	175.00		50.00	175.00		
Creamer	125.00		35.00	115.00		
Spooner	125.00		40.00	90.00		
Sunk Hollyhock						
Bowl Rare				60.00*		
Surf Spray						
Pickle Dish	45.00	40.00	25.00			

	Blue	Green	White	Vaseline Canary	Cranberry	Other
Swag With Brackets						
Pitcher	275.00	260.00	185.00	250.00		
Tumbler	75.00	50.00	30.00	55.00		
Butter	250.00	235.00	190.00	225.00		
Sugar	125.00	125.00	50.00	100.00		
Creamer	75.00	65.00	40.00	70.00		
Spooner	125.00	125.00	80.00	120.00		
Bowl, Master	70.00	60.00	38.00	65.00		
Bowl, Sauce	30.00	26.00	16.00	25.00		
Toothpick Holder	300.00	270.00	200.00	285.00		
Shakers, pair	185.00	165.00	125.00	175.00		
Cruet	460.00	290.00	135.00	195.00		
Jelly Compote	48.00	35.00	20.00	45.00		
Novelty Bowl	45.00	38.00	18.00	40.00		
Swastika						
Pitcher	295.00	275.00	175.00		325.00	
Tumbler	75.00	65.00	50.00		100.00	
Syrup	500.00	550.00	440.00		600.00	
Snowflake						
Night Lamp	1,200.00*		750.00*		1,700.00	
Hand Lamp	350.00*		250.00*		595.00	
Oil Lamp	290.00*		175.00*		495.00	
Swirling Maze						
Pitcher, either (avg)	250.00	240.00	105.00		500.00	
Tumbler	50.00	40.00	18.00		90.00	
Salad Bowl	85.00	70.00	40.00		135.00	
S-Repeat						
Pitcher	450.00*		300.00*			
Tumbler	50.00		30.00			
Bowl, Master	75.00	85.00	50.00			
Swirl						
Pitcher	125.00	120.00	60.00	275.00	595.00	
Tumbler	25.00	22.00	12.00	40.00	95.00	
Butter	120.00	115.00	60.00		145.00	
Sugar	85.00	90.00	44.00		160.00	
Creamer	60.00	65.00	32.00		85.00	
Spooner	60.00	70.00	30.00		125.00	
Bowl, Master	40.00	45.00	30.00		65.00	
Bowl, Sauce	18.00	20.00	12.00		28.00	
Syrup	105.00	100.00	65.00		140.00	
Sugar Shaker	125.00	90.00	57.00		150.00	
Cruet, 2 sizes	150.00	185.00	85.00		265.00	
Shakers, pair	160.00	125.00	86.00		225.00	
Fingerbowl	50.00	52.00	29.00		75.00	
Toothpick Holder	95.00	100.00	60.00		95.00	
Mustard Jar	85.00	90.00	42.00		130.00	
Rosebowl	50.00	55.00	28.00		70.00	

	Blue	Green	White	Vaseline Canary	Cranberry	Other
Swirl(Continued)						
Celery Vase	70.00	75.00	40.00		130.00	
Custard Cup	40.00	45.00	26.00		65.00	
Water, Bitters & Bar						
Bottles, each	85.00-195.00	80.00-160.00	60.00-95.00		300.00-395.00	
Lampshade	90.00	80.00	30.00		175.00	
Cheese Dish			210.00		350.00	
Fingerlamp			310.00		560.00	
Cruet Set, Complete					430.00	
Vase (Fenton)					130.00	
Strawholder rare	700.00*		500.00*		1,000.00	
Scottish Moor (English)						
Pitcher	300.00		200.00		450.00	375.00 Rubina
						350.00 Amethyst
Tumbler	70.00		60.00		90.00	80.00 Amethyst
						90.00 Rubina
Cruet	350.00*		200.00*			
Cracker Jar	325.00*		185.00*			
Celery Vase	110.00*		85.00*			
Target						
Vase		90.00*				
Thistle Patch						
Novelty, Footed			28.00			
Thousand Eye						
Pitcher			80.00			
Tumbler			20.00			
Butter			115.00			
Sugar			80.00			
Creamer			65.00			
Spooner			65.00			
Celery Vase			80.00			
Cruet			120.00			
Shakers, pair			65.00			
Toothpick Holder			110.00			
Bottles, Various			18.00-30.00			
Bowl, Various			15.00-30.00			
Three Fruits						
Bowl	70.00		45.00			
Three Fruits w/Meander						
Bowl, Footed	75.00		50.00			
Three Fingers & Panel						
Bowl, Master rare	85.00		60.00	80.00		
Bowl, Sauce rare	25.00		16.00	20.00		

	Blue	Green	White	Vaseline Canary	Cranberry	Other
Tiny Tears						
Vase	40.00	35.00	20.00			
Tokyo*						
Pitcher	300.00	280.00	150.00			
Tumbler	70.00	60.00	40.00			
Butter	175.00	160.00	80.00			
Sugar	110.00	125.00	55.00			
Creamer	65.00	60.00	35.00			
Spooner	80.00	75.00	40.00			
Vase	50.00	45.00	30.00			
Cruet	175.00	170.00	85.00			
Syrup	140.00	130.00	65.00			
Jelly Compote	40.00	35.00	25.00			
Plate	55.00	50.00	30.00			
Bowl, Master	40.00	28.00	15.00			
Bowl, Sauce	20.00	14.00	10.00			
Shakers, pair	80.00	70.00	40.00			
Toothpick Holder	200.00	180.00	115.00			
Trailing Vine						
Novelty Bowl	45.00		30.00	40.00		
Tree of Love						
Novelty Bowl			27.00			
Compote			30.00			
Tree Stump						
Mug		55.00	50.00	30.00		
Tree Trunk						
Vase	35.00	30.00	20.00			
Twig						
Vase, Small	50.00	70.00	35.00			
Vase, Panelled	60.00	60.00				
Twist (miniatures)						
Butter	250.00*		150.00*	225.00*		
Sugar	125.00*		65.00*	120.00*		
Creamer	75.00*		35.00*	70.00*		
Spooner	80.00*		40.00*	75.00*		
Twisted Ribs						
Vase	30.00	26.00	18.00			
Twister						
Bowl	40.00	36.00	24.00			
Venetian (Spider Web)						
Vase	40.00					

	Blue	Green	White	Vaseline Canary	Cranberry	Other
Vintage						
Novelty Bowl	38.00	36.00	26.00			
War of The Roses (English)						
Novelty Bowl	55.00			50.00		
Waterlily & Cattails						
Pitcher	395.00	345.00	230.00			395.00 Amethyst
Tumbler	55.00	45.00	20.00			60.00 Amethyst
Butter	375.00	330.00	200.00			395.00 Amethyst
Sugar	175.00	140.00	90.00			195.00 Amethyst
Creamer	47.00	40.00	30.00			55.00 Amethyst
Spooner	50.00	42.00	30.00			65.00 Amethyst
Bowl, Master	55.00	50.00	35.00			60.00 Amethyst
Bowl, Sauce	28.00	24.00	25.00			30.00 Amethyst
Novelty Bowl	36.00	30.00	24.00			40.00 Amethyst
Bon Bon	58.00	45.00	30.00			65.00 Amethyst
Relish, Handled	80.00	75.00	50.00			90.00 Amethyst
Plate	75.00	70.00	46.00			80.00 Amethyst
Breakfast Set, 2 pieces	120.00	110.00	70.00			135.00 Amethyst
Gravy Boat, handled	55.00	47.00	55.00			60.00 Amethyst
Wheel & Block						
Novelty Bowl	36.00	34.00	25.00			
Vase Whimsey	30.00	28.00	18.00			
Wild Bouquet						
Pitcher	250.00	195.00	120.00			
Tumbler	100.00	65.00	22.00			
Butter	450.00	350.00	270.00			
Sugar	200.00	175.00	125.00			
Creamer	75.00	70.00	40.00			
Spooner	125.00	90.00	80.00			
Bowl, Master	125.00	110.00	80.00			
Bowl, Sauce	35.00	30.00	20.00			
Cruet	300.00	350.00	110.00			
Toothpick Holder	350.00	250.00	175.00			
Shakers, pair	90.00	80.00	55.00			
Cruet Set w/tray	395.00	360.00	240.00			
Jelly Compote	125.00	100.00	60.00			
Wide Panel						
Epergne, 4 Lily	200.00*	185.00*	130.00*			
Wild Rose						
Mug	28.00		20.00			
Novelty Bowl	38.00		25.00			
Banana Bowl	40.00		25.00			
William & Mary (English)						
Creamer	50.00			45.00		

	Blue	Green	White	Vaseline Canary	Cranberry	Other
William & Mary (English) (Continued)						
Open Sugar	50.00			40.00		
Master Salt	40.00			30.00		
Compote	65.00			60.00		
Windflower						
Bowl rare	65.00		50.00			
Windows (Plain)						
Pitcher, Various	125.00		96.00		400.00	
Tumbler	40.00		28.00		90.00	
Mini Lamp	135.00				1,700.00	
Finger Bowl	45.00		38.00		50.00	
Oil Lamp					500.00	
Shade	45.00		28.00		155.00	
Windows (Swirled)						
Pitcher, Various	350.00		260.00		695.00	
Tumbler	75.00		50.00		100.00	
Butter	375.00		280.00		500.00	
Sugar	210.00		120.00		300.00	
Creamer	80.00		50.00		200.00	
Spooner	80.00		50.00		150.00	
Bowl, Master	45.00		30.00		70.00	
Bowl, Sauce	25.00		18.00		40.00	
Toothpick Holder	275.00		150.00		300.00	
Mustard Jar	65.00		40.00		100.00	
Cruet	275.00		195.00		400.00	
Sugar Shaker	135.00		95.00		300.00	
Syrup, 2 shapes	275.00		175.00		450.00	
Shakers, pair	140.00		65.00		250.00	
Cruet Set	225.00		100.00		495.00	
Celery Vase	75.00		39.00		140.00	
Plate, 2 sizes	80.00		40.00		200.00	
Barber Bottle					275.00	
Wilted Flowers						
Bowl	30.00	35.00	18.00			
Winged Scroll						
Nappy rare				130.00		
Winter Cabbage						
Novelty Bowl, Ftd.	45.00	40.00	30.00			
Winterlily						
Vase, Ftd			30.00			
Wishbone & Drapery						
Novelty Bowl	35.00	30.00	25.00			

	Blue	Green	White	Vaseline Canary	Cranberry	Other
Woven Wonder						
Rosebowl	40.00		30.00			
Novelty Bowl	45.00		27.00			
Wreath & Shell						
Pitcher	550.00		170.00	340.00	600.00	
Tumbler, Flat or Ftd.	90.00		35.00	50.00	80.00	
Butter	225.00		115.00	190.00	195.00	
Sugar	180.00		55.00	130.00	130.00	
Creamer	125.00		60.00	80.00	85.00	
Spooner	125.00		60.00	65.00	70.00	
Bowl, Master	85.00		55.00	95.00	110.00	
Bowl, Sauce	30.00		18.00	20.00	30.00	
Celery Vase	165.00		95.00	150.00	170.00	
Rosebowl	80.00		60.00	75.00	110.00	
Toothpick Holder	250.00		175.00	250.00	260.00	
Ladies Spittoon	75.00		50.00	95.00	90.00	
Cracker Jar	560.00		410.00	500.00	750.00	
Salt Dip	115.00		60.00	80.00	85.00	
Novelty Bowl	60.00		40.00	50.00	60.00	

Note: add 15% for decorated items.

	Blue	Green	White	Vaseline Canary	Cranberry	Other
Zipper & Loops						
Vase, footed	45.00	40.00	30.00			

Items Pictured on Pages 5-27 not listed above.

	Blue	Green	White	Vaseline Canary	Cranberry	Other
Divilbis						
Atomizer						30.00 Cobalt
Duncan & Miller						
Freeform bowl	50.00					
Fenton Hobnail						
Lamp	500.00					
Fenton Swan						
Bowl	175.00					
Hobnail						
Spittoon					200.00	
Vase			20.00			
Hobnail Variant W/Zipper Mould						
Vase			25.00			
Rustic Hobnail						
Handled Basket			95.00			
Waffle						
Epergne						750.00 Olive & Pink

Schroeder's Antiques Price Guide

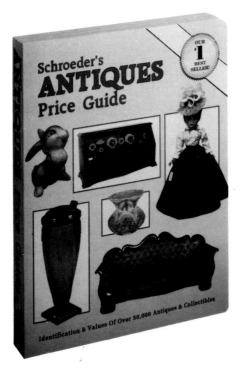

Schroeder's Antiques Price Guide has become THE household name in the antiques & collectibles field. Our team of editors works year-round with more than 200 contributors to bring you our #1 best-selling book on antiques & collectibles.

With more than 50,000 items identified & priced, Schroeder's is a must for the collector & dealer alike. If it merits the interest of today's collector, you'll find it in Schroeder's. Each subject is represented with histories and background information. In addition, hundreds of sharp original photos are used each year to illustrate not only the rare and unusual, but the everyday "fun-type" collectibles as well — not postage stamp pictures, but large close-up shots that show important details clearly.

Our editors compile a new book each year. Never do we merely change prices. Accuracy is our primary aim. Prices are gathered over the entire year previous to publication, from ads and personal contacts. Then each category is thoroughly checked to spot inconsistencies, listings that may not be entirely reflective of actual market dealings, and lines too vague to be of merit. Only the best of the lot remains for publication. You'll find Schroeder's Antiques Price Guide the one to buy for factual information and quality.

No dealer, collector or investor can afford not to own this book. It is available from your favorite bookseller or antiques dealer at the low price of $12.95. If you are unable to find this price guide in your area, it's available from Collector Books, P.O. Box 3009, Paducah, KY 42002-3009 at $12.95 plus $2.00 for postage and handling.

8½ x 11", 608 Pages   **$12.95**

COLLECTOR BOOKS
A Division of Schroeder Publishing Co., Inc.